Big Data

COLLECTION

STRATEGIES TO REDUCE COSTS AND MAXIMIZE INVESTMENT

BIG DATA

Prof. Marcão - Marcus Vinícius Pinto

Disclaimer:

Please note that the information contained in this document is for educational and entertainment purposes only. Every effort has been made to provide complete, accurate, up-to-date, and reliable information. No warranty of any kind is express or implied.

By reading this text, the reader agrees that under no circumstances is the author liable for any losses, direct or indirect, incurred as a result of the use of the information contained in this book, including, but not limited to, errors, omissions, or inaccuracies.

ISBN: 9798311668040

Publishing imprint: Independently published

Summary.

1   Foreword.

Welcome to a deep dive into the universe of Big Data and the strategies that turn high costs into optimized investments. This book, "Strategies for Reducing Costs and Maximizing Big Data Investments," is part of the "Big Data" collection for sale on Amazon, a series designed to empower professionals to navigate the complexities of the data age safely and efficiently.

Here, you won't just find abstract theories or empty promises. This is a practical handbook, packed with in-depth analysis, real-world case studies, and proven strategies to help you navigate the complex Big Data ecosystem. Whether you are an IT manager, a data analyst, an entrepreneur or a business professional, this book is designed for you.

1.1   Who is this book written for?

This book is intended for professionals who understand that Big Data is a powerful tool, but who also recognize the need to balance investments with tangible returns. It was written to:

- IT managers and CIOs: who seek to optimize Big Data infrastructure, reducing costs without compromising security or performance.

- Data Analysts and Data Scientists: who want to understand how the cost structure impacts their analytics and how they can contribute to more cost-effective decisions.

- Entrepreneurs and Small Business Owners: Who need to implement Big Data solutions in an affordable and scalable way, without compromising their budget.

- Business and Strategy Professionals: who need to align investments in Big Data with the organization's strategic objectives, maximizing the return on investment (ROI).

- Students and Academics: who seek a practical and applicable view of the economic challenges of Big Data, complementing their theoretical training.

1.2   What will you find in this book?

Throughout these pages, we will explore the key components of Big Data infrastructure, from data collection and storage to processing and analysis. We will discuss the initial and ongoing costs, including storage, processing clusters, software licensing, and specialized labor.

You'll also find chapters devoted to critical topics such as:

- Management and Maintenance: How to balance the costs of human capital, security, and data governance.

- Hidden Costs: Identifying and mitigating expenses that often go unnoticed.

- Big Data for Small Businesses: Affordable strategies for those who don't have the budget of a multinational.

- Cloud Cost Analysis: Understanding the trade-offs between public, private, and hybrid cloud.

- Data Disposal and Deactivation: How to ensure that the end of the data lifecycle is secure and cost-effective.

In addition, the book addresses emerging technology trends such as automation, artificial intelligence, and cloud computing, showing how they can be used to reduce costs and increase efficiency.

1.3   Why Is This Book Different?

What makes this book unique is its balanced approach between theory and practice. We do not just present problems; We offer solutions.

Each chapter is built on up-to-date research, real-world examples, and strategies that you can implement right away.

In addition, the book was written in an accessible language, but without losing academic rigor. Our goal is for you, the reader, to be able to grasp complex concepts without feeling overwhelmed, while also being challenged to think critically about how to apply this knowledge in your professional context.

1.4   Why invest in this collection?

This book is part of the "Big Data" collection, a series that sets out to cover all aspects of this ever-evolving field. By purchasing this collection, you will have access to a set of works that complement each other, offering a 360-degree view of Big Data — from the technical fundamentals to the strategic and economic implications.

If you want to become a professional in the field of artificial intelligence and Big Data, this collection is the right investment. Each book has been carefully crafted to provide real value, helping you stand out in an increasingly competitive market.

The Big Data revolution is in full swing, and this book is your passport to participate in it strategically and efficiently. Get ready for an engaging, challenging and, above all, transformative read.

Happy reading and happy discoveries!

Prof. Marcão - Marcus Vinícius Pinto

M.Sc. in Information Technology
Specialist in Information Technology.
Consultant, Mentor and Speaker on Artificial Intelligence,
Information Architecture and Data Governance.
Founder, CEO, teacher and
pedagogical advisor at MVP Consult.

2   Speaking of Costs.

After collection and analysis, Big Data will provide ways to solve existing challenges and also subsidize solutions to problems that have not yet been identified. Although companies are aware of the potential of Big Data to solve previously unsolvable problems, the process comes at a high cost.

Operational processes, as discussed earlier, will need to be changed to accommodate Big Data. New data types will need to be added to the environment. In addition, new types of analytics will emerge to help understand the implications of Big Data and how it relates or does not relate to existing data (Widjaya, 2019)

To understand the financial impact of costs and investments to have Big Data in the company, it is necessary to examine the constraints for it to produce results. This examination shall consider:

- The identification of the data sources that will be handled by Big Data.

- The impact on the company's processes by modifications to already established business processes or by the creation of new processes.

- The changes in technology or new technologies that will be necessary to incorporate Big Data into the company's technology park.

- The search and acquisition of new talent and upgrades to existing talent.

- The ROI potential of Big Data investments.

It is also necessary to examine these constraints from two perspectives and try to understand the relationship between the economic impacts and the advantages of Big Data:

- – The costs to deploy Big Data.

- – The costs to keep Big Data operational.

Big Data infrastructure involves a wide range of technological components and capabilities that are essential for operating complex data platforms. These elements work in synergy to collect, store, process, and transmit large volumes of data in an efficient, secure, and scalable manner.

2.1   Key Components of Big Data Infrastructure.

2.1.1   Data Collection.

The first step in the Big Data flow is the capture of raw data. This can be accomplished through IoT sensors, monitoring devices, social media APIs, internal company systems, or specialized extraction and tracking tools. This data can include system logs, transactional data, mobile device information, and real-time streams.

2.1.2   Data Storage.

After collection, a robust system is required to store the data securely and affordably. Among the most common options are database management systems (DBMS), data warehouses, and data lakes. Storage can be on-premises, cloud, or hybrid, depending on the company's needs.

 - Data lakes are widely used to store structured and unstructured data, offering flexibility for future analysis.

- Data warehouses, on the other hand, are optimized for structured queries and enterprise analytics.

2.1.3   Processing and Analysis.

To extract value from data, it is essential to have advanced processing and analysis tools, such as Hadoop, Spark, Apache Cassandra, and Kafka. These platforms allow you to perform large-scale analysis, implement machine learning algorithms, and derive strategic insights in a timely manner.

2.1.4   Computer Network.

The interconnection of all components requires an efficient network, with high-speed technologies, routers, switches, and secure protocols for data transmission. Minimal latency and reliability are crucial aspects for the success of the operation.

2.1.5   Security and Data Protection,

With cyber threats on the rise, it is imperative to implement robust security systems such as firewalls, encryption, and role-based access control (RBAC). Compliance with regulations, such as LGPD (General Data Protection Law) in Brazil, is also essential.

2.1.6   Scalability and Virtualization.

The ability to flexibly expand resources by utilizing technologies such as containers (Docker, Kubernetes) and cloud services is critical to meeting growing data demand.

2.2   Startup Costs of Big Data Infrastructure[1].

Implementing a Big Data infrastructure requires significant investments in hardware, software, and technical expertise. The following are some of the main costs involved:

---

[1] Estimated values at 01/2025.

2.2.1   Storage.

The cost of storage varies depending on the capacity and type of solution chosen. For on-premises solutions, the average estimate is $1,000 to $2,000 per terabyte (TB). A 1 petabyte (PB) storage system can cost around $1 million, considering the need for redundancy and fault tolerance.

Alternatively, cloud solutions such as AWS S3, Google Cloud Storage, or Azure Blob offer usage-based pricing, typically between $0.02 to $0.23 per GB/month, depending on access frequency and performance requirements.

2.2.2   Processing Clusters (Hadoop and Spark).

A Hadoop cluster requires a minimum of three nodes to ensure fault tolerance. Each node is usually a medium-sized server, with an estimated cost of between $4,000 and $6,000, offering 3TB to 6TB of storage. For a 1 PB cluster, approximately 200 nodes would be required, bringing the total cost to about $1 million.

2.2.3   Network Costs.

High-speed networks and equipment such as state-of-the-art routers and switches are essential. Setting up a suitable network infrastructure can range from $10,000 to $50,000, depending on the scale.

2.2.4   Software Licensing.

 While Hadoop and Spark are open source, additional Big Data tools such as Tableau, Databricks, or specific machine learning solutions may incur licensing costs ranging from $10,000 to $100,000 per year.

Security solutions, such as monitoring systems and data protection, also add operational costs.

2.2.5   Labor and Expertise.

A skilled team is crucial for designing, implementing, and managing the infrastructure. Data engineers, data scientists, and specialized systems administrators can cost, on average, $100,000 to $150,000 annually per professional, depending on location and experience.

2.3   To be aware.

Investing in a Big Data infrastructure is strategic for companies that want to take advantage of the benefits of advanced data analytics. However, it is essential to carry out careful planning, considering not only the initial costs but also the recurring investments in maintenance, upgrades, and scalability. Adopting modern solutions, combined with a data-driven approach, can provide a significant payoff over time.

It is recommended that each of these clusters be at least a mid-range Intel server, which costs[2] between $4,000 and $6,000 for 3TB and 6TB of disk space. A good rule of thumb is to assume that it will cost $1,000 - $2,000 per TB. A 1-petabyte Hadoop cluster will cost around $1 million since it needs around 200 nodes.

[2] Values calculated in September 2019.

3 The cost of management and maintenance.

The initial cost of acquiring a big data management system is only a fraction of the total investment required to implement and maintain an efficient big data infrastructure. While purchasing or licensing specific software may require an upfront outlay, the ongoing costs associated with managing and maintaining that system are critical to ensuring its proper functioning and making the most of its potential.

The management of a Big Data system involves a series of fundamental activities, such as the continuous integration of new data sources, the cleaning and transformation of data, the configuration and adjustment of processing and analysis processes, as well as the constant monitoring of the infrastructure to ensure its performance and stability.

In addition, maintaining a Big Data system requires continuous attention to security updates and fixes, performance and capacity enhancements, as well as keeping up with the development of new technologies and methodologies in the field of Big Data. This usually requires a specialized team dedicated to system administration and technical support.

The complexity and scale of Big Data systems can also come with additional costs, such as the need for large-scale data storage resources, high-performance servers, robust network infrastructure, and advanced security measures. These costs can include investments in hardware, additional software, software licenses, cloud services, and even hiring external experts.

It is also important to consider that the analysis and use of Big Data data requires specialized skills and knowledge, which may involve training and training for the internal team, or even the hiring of specialized consultants and professionals.

In this way, the total cost of Big Data goes far beyond the initial investment in the management system. It covers recurring management and maintenance costs, as well as ongoing investments in hardware, software, security, training, and technical support.

It is also important to consider indirect costs, such as the time and resources required to implement and integrate the Big Data system into the company's existing operations.

It is essential to understand that the management and maintenance of a Big Data system requires an ongoing commitment to ensuring the quality and reliability of the data. This involves adopting data governance practices, implementing cybersecurity policies, constantly monitoring data integrity, and ensuring compliance with applicable regulations and standards.

Another fundamental aspect is the constant evolution of the Big Data system. As the demands and needs of the company change, it is necessary to adapt the system to ensure that it continues to meet objectives and expectations. This may involve expanding storage capacity, improving data processing performance, incorporating new technologies and advanced analytics techniques, among others.

It is important to note that the total cost of Big Data can vary significantly according to the size and complexity of the company, the amount of data to be processed, the technological resources required, among other factors. Therefore, it is necessary to make a careful analysis of the costs involved and carry out strategic planning to maximize the return on investment.

The additional costs begin to accumulate to the original value as soon as the company feels the need to adjust the sizing of its operations. Once a 6 TB cluster may need to scale up to more than 200 petabytes of storage space, handling hundreds of thousands of nodes.

This presents an even bigger problem than simply paying for the cost of additional storage space and processing power.

More infrastructure means that more people are needed to manage it, which brings us to the more variable cost implication of adopting a big data platform.

3.1   The cost of human capital.

The technology segment is one of the fastest evolving sectors there is. As a direct result, data science has quickly exploded into one of the most popular career options for new university graduates.

However, being a relatively new field means that there are not as many professionals to make it as accessible as in other sectors.

A full-time Hadoop specialist will cost between $90,000 and $180,000 per year, while outsourced work costs an average of $81-$100 per hour. The cost of development varies greatly depending on the developer's experience, their location, and the size of the project.

Business analysts will need to consider growing their ranks with data scientists. This can be accomplished with consulting support in the startup phases but should evolve into a permanent team as the direction and benefits become clearer.

Hiring a single data scientist doesn't seem like a good answer. Unless your company is medium-sized and does not have many products and situations to be analyzed.

Better results will be achieved by creating a team of data scientists tasked with discovering Big Data sources, analyzing analytical processes, and managing impacts on business processes (Davenport, 2014) (Davenport et al., 2012).

For the IT team, knowledge of new Big Data technologies will need to be introduced to the existing ones in the teams through training and mentoring. Consulting resources can and should be employed to help your company get started with its Big Data initiatives.

Data scientists are responsible for modeling complex business problems, uncovering business insights, and identifying opportunities.

They bring to work:

- Ability to integrate and prepare large and varied data sets

- Advanced analysis and modeling skills to reveal and understand dark relationships

- Business knowledge to apply a context

- Communication skills to present results

Data science is an emerging field. Demand is high, and finding qualified personnel is one of the main challenges associated with Big Data analysis. A data scientist may be based in IT or in the business – but wherever he or she is, he or she will be your new best friend and collaborator in planning and implementing Big Data analytics projects (Davenport et al., 2012).

Data science is an interdisciplinary area, consisting of computer science, mathematics, and statistics, and the specialization of the domain in which the data derives.

The goal of data science is to harness the power of data to gain valuable insights and turn them into knowledge that underpins rational decision-making. To achieve this goal, a diverse set of skills and knowledge is required, which cover areas such as mathematics, statistics, programming, and mastery of the field of study in which the data is being analyzed.

A data scientist is a highly valued and sought-after professional in today's market due to their ability to extract meaningful information from data. This professional needs to have solid knowledge in mathematics and statistics to understand the statistical methods and techniques applicable to data analysis. In addition, mastery of programming is essential for handling large volumes of data and applying machine learning algorithms and statistical modeling techniques.

However, finding a professional with this skill set and expertise can be challenging, as the demand for data scientists significantly outstrips the supply of skilled professionals. This scarcity creates a rarity in today's market.

Not only do data scientists possess advanced technical knowledge, but they also need to be analytically minded and able to formulate appropriate questions to guide their analyses. They must have communication skills to translate complex results into understandable insights for decision-makers. The ability to lead projects and work in a team is also important, as data science often involves collaboration with experts in different fields.

The market is increasingly aware of the importance of data science and is investing in the training and development of these rare professionals. Universities, online courses, and training programs are popping up to meet the demand for data science specialists.

The skills required by a data scientist can be divided into seven categories:

1. Programming. The main programming languages used are Python and R. Another highly requested computer knowledge is SQL.

2. Work with data. It boils down to collecting, cleaning, and transforming data to be used.

3. Descriptive statistics. Application of various techniques to describe and summarize a dataset.

4. Data visualization. Knowledge and use of tools to transform data into interpretable graphs.

5. Statistical model. Creation of statistical models and use of them for statistical inference and hypothesis testing.

6. Dealing with Big Data. Using tools required due to the large volumes of data handled.

7. Machine learning. Knowledge and creation of Machine Learning algorithms for decision making and prediction.

The main tools that a data scientist uses are presented in the following figure.

In almost all polls, these two tend to be tied in terms of popularity. However, both languages have their strengths and weaknesses.

On the X-axis, we have the name of the tool, which includes programming languages, data platforms, or analysis tools. On the Y-axis, we have the percentage of respondents who report that they use the corresponding tool.

As we can see, the most used tool is SQL. The next tool is Excel, a simple yet very powerful tool. Then, there are two programming languages tied Python and R. These two languages are the darlings of the Data Science world.

And what is the data scientist's job like? We can summarize this work in 6 activities presented in the following figure.

The Data Science process works like this:

1st. A question, yet to be answered, needs to be found. It can be a hypothesis that needs to be tested, a decision that needs to be made, or something that one wants to try to predict.

2nd. The data is collected for analysis. Sometimes this means designing an experiment to create new data, other times the data already exists and you need to find it.

3rd. The data collected is prepared for analysis. It is a process usually referred to as data munging or data wrangling. In this process, the data is cleaned and transformed into a format suitable for analysis.

4th. A template is created for the data. In the most generic sense, this can be a numerical model, a visual model, a statistical model, or a machine learning model. Once created, the model is used to provide evidence for or against a hypothesis, to help decide or predict an outcome.

5th. The model is validated. It is determined whether the model answers the question, helps with decision-making, or returns an accurate prediction. In addition, it is necessary to ratify whether the model created is appropriate, considering the data and context.

6th. The model is deployed. This may mean communicating the results of the analysis to others, deciding and taking action, or putting an application into production.

Data science can be thought of as an ongoing process. The cycle described above is repeated several times and with each iteration learnings and improvements are implemented in the model. It is interesting to note that the process is often not sequential, it is often necessary to skip steps back or forth, as problems arise and learnings about better solutions are discovered.

3.2   The costs of Data Security and Governance.

Data Security and Governance play a key role in the Big Data landscape, where the quantity, variety, and velocity of data generated and processed are increasing. Protecting data from cyber threats, complying with data protection regulations, and applying appropriate governance practices are essential to ensuring data integrity, confidentiality, and availability.

When it comes to implementing cybersecurity measures in the context of Big Data, it's crucial to take a comprehensive approach and layers of defense in depth. This involves the use of firewalls, data encryption, intrusion detection systems, access control, and authentication, among other security measures. In addition, implementing data security practices at every stage of the data collection, storage, processing, and sharing process is critical to protecting sensitive information from theft, leaks, or unauthorized breaches.

Regarding compliance with data protection regulations, companies must ensure that they are compliant with applicable laws and standards, such as the GDPR in the European Union or the LGPD in Brazil. This involves appointing a data protection officer, conducting data protection impact assessments, implementing appropriate technical and organizational security measures, and ensuring the rights of data subjects, such as the right to privacy and the right to be forgotten.

Data governance in the context of Big Data is another crucial aspect of ensuring the proper and effective use of data. Defining clear data management policies, standardizing metadata, creating data catalogs, monitoring data performance, and data quality are all practices that contribute to robust data governance. In addition, implementing data governance processes allows organizations to maximize the value of data, reduce exposure risks, and ensure compliance with current regulations.

A practical example of effective implementation of data security and governance in the context of Big Data can be observed in a financial institution. In this highly regulated and sensitive landscape, the use of advanced cybersecurity technologies, such as next-generation firewalls, encryption of data at rest and in transit, and continuous threat monitoring, is essential to protect the confidentiality and integrity of customers' financial information.

Additionally, implementing a robust data governance program that includes setting clear data management policies, creating consistent metadata, and establishing a data governance committee, helps to ensure that data is managed ethically, securely, and in compliance with financial industry laws and regulations.

3.3   Miscellaneous big data costs.

The factors presented so far provide a good representation of how much Big Data costs, but the question does not stop there, most of the time. The cost of the factors that fall under this section mainly depend on the particularities of the company.

Among them, the following can be mentioned.

3.3.1   Legacy technology and migration costs.

The rapid evolution of technology has led many companies to face challenges related to legacy technology and migration costs. A notable example of this situation concerns Hadoop, a platform for processing large volumes of data that many experts consider to be becoming obsolete. However, for companies that already have Hadoop integrated into their data pipelines, migrating to new solutions can be a complex and costly task.

Reliance on legacy technology puts companies in a position of vulnerability, since business demands and requirements are constantly evolving. The adoption of new software solutions becomes essential to meet new challenges and remain competitive in the market.

The costs involved in migrating from legacy technology to more modern solutions constitute another significant challenge. In addition to the high financial investments required, migration can also require a large training and reskilling effort for internal teams. This can impact on the company's operational efficiency during the transition process.

However, it is crucial for companies to consider the long-term benefits of migrating to new technological solutions. By adopting the most up-to-date technologies, organizations can gain competitive advantages, such as improvements in agility, scalability, and performance. In addition, updating the technological infrastructure can enable the adoption of new business strategies, allowing the incorporation of advanced data analysis, artificial intelligence, and machine learning.

3.3.2 Network costs.

The average business often underestimates the impact of network costs on their operations. While the cost of transferring data over the Internet may seem low and insignificant for small amounts of data, it changes dramatically when dealing with large volumes of information.

For companies that handle terabytes or even petabytes of data, bandwidth costs can quickly become significant. As the demand for data transfer increases, whether through uploads, downloads, streaming, or any other form of online communication, network spending begins to pile up.

These costs can come from different sources, such as internet providers or cloud services used for data storage and transfer. Depending on the specifics of the contract and the needs of the company, bandwidth can become an important expense to be considered in the budget.

In addition, it is worth mentioning that network costs are not limited to data transfer only. It is also necessary to consider the costs related to maintaining, updating, and expanding the company's network infrastructure. This implies investments in equipment, servers, routers, firewalls, and other components necessary to ensure a reliable and secure network.

Given this, it is essential for companies to make an in-depth analysis of their network costs and adopt efficient strategies to optimize these expenses. This may involve implementing more efficient data management policies, such as compression and deduplication, using caching technologies, monitoring network traffic to identify bottlenecks and inefficiencies, among others.

3.3.3 Proxy providers.

When it comes to collecting data from the web as part of a Big Data strategy, it is important to consider the cost of proxy providers. Proxy providers play an essential role by allowing businesses to collect large amounts of data efficiently and without overloading the target servers. However, these services often come at an associated cost, especially as the amount of data collected increases.

When using web scraping, the process of automated data collection, it is common for businesses to make multiple requests over time. Each request involves interaction with the proxy provider, which redirects the request to the desired web server and returns the collected data. Depending on the volume of requests and the size of the data collected, the proxy provider's monthly bill can increase significantly.

Given this scenario, it is important for companies to make a careful selection of the proxy provider, considering their needs and budget. There are several tools available in the market that help you compare the features and prices offered by the various providers. These tools can consider factors such as the number of requests allowed, connection speed, quality of technical support, and scalability options.

By choosing the proper proxy provider, businesses can ensure efficient utilization of resources and avoid unpleasant surprises on monthly bills. Additionally, it is critical to conduct a periodic analysis of the costs involved in using proxy providers, as data needs and volumes can change over time.

3.3.4   Data preservation costs.

When it comes to preserving data, we often don't realize the cost involved in this process. Taking regular snapshots of data is essential to ensure the security and integrity of the information stored, but it also comes with additional costs.

One of the most common options for data preservation is the creation of regular backups, which can be made both on physical devices and on cloud storage services. However, these backups incur costs, both in terms of additional storage required and in terms of the computational resources used during the process of creating backups.

In addition, depending on the amount of data and the frequency of creating backups, costs can increase significantly. This is especially true for companies that deal with large volumes of data or that need to comply with specific regulations regarding data preservation.

Another important factor to consider is the costs of recovering data in case of loss or failures. If an incident occurs and data needs to be restored from backups, additional resources will be required to perform this recovery. This may involve specialized services, such as hiring data recovery consultants, or allocating time and in-house resources to deal with the issue.

To properly account for data preservation costs, it is essential to take into account all related aspects, such as the additional storage required, the computational resources used to create backups, and the possibility of additional costs in case of data recovery.

Companies should conduct a careful analysis of their data preservation requirements and determine the best strategy that meets their needs while also being economically viable. This may involve adopting more efficient storage and backup technologies, allocating resources appropriately, and creating data preservation policies that balance security with cost.

3.4   Hidden Costs of Big Data.

Unfortunately, the considerations about the costs of Big Data do not end with the items discussed in the previous section. If you stop your calculations without considering the items discussed in this section, you will not have a comprehensive analysis of the true cost of data management operations.

The main sources of hidden costs are:

1   Inefficient data integration.

Deriving value from enterprise data typically requires it to be transformed and integrated. If the data integration solution adopted by the company involves a lot of manual effort, redundancy, or other types of inefficiency, it can be a major source of hidden costs in the form of wasted staff time and unnecessary infrastructure.

2   Unnecessary backups.

File storage can be simple and inexpensive for the typical PC user - he has a few hundred GB of documents, photos, and videos on his hard drive. Things are much more expensive and complicated in a company. A business has a lot more files to deal with, and it needs to make sure that those files are safe.

Backup, recovery, and archiving are the most important storage technology segments among organizations. Backups are even more popular than virtualization and cloud computing.

The company should always back up its data. However, if you're backing up your data more often than you need to, or storing more copies than you need, you may not be operating as cost-effectively as possible.

You need to be sure that the right level of data backups are being performed, but not more.

3   Low-quality data.

Data riddled with quality issues is likely to cost much more to store, integrate, and analyze than error-free data. While avoiding data quality issues entirely may not be possible, fixing data quality issues through automated tools can help you minimize the costs you incur due to poor data quality.

4   Uninformed employees

Are the data scientists on your team conscientious professionals? Or do they totally lack an understanding of data management's best practices?

In the latter case, a lack of commitment and dedication can increase Big Data costs, creating bottlenecks and data quality errors whenever someone who is not a professional data scientist touches the data.

Avoid this hidden cost of big data by turning your employees into collaborating data scientists.

3.4.1   Alleviating the great cost of Big Data.

A big data platform is very expensive to manage for the average business, but this cost can be greatly reduced in many ways. The most important of these is to leverage managed and open-source Big Data platforms.

One of the consequences of the popularity of cloud-based software is the proliferation of proprietary, managed, and open-source software. This is opposed to licensed and on-premises solutions, respectively.

As Big Data matures, it will be necessary to consider new evolving data types and new data sources. Some of them can be controlled, while others will control some of what is done.

The most important decisions that need to be made regarding types and sources are:

- How often will it be necessary to interact with the data?

- Is it possible to trust the data sources and the data themselves?

- What can be done with the data?

- What data will be needed to address your business problem?

- Who retains ownership of the data and the products of the work?

- How long is it necessary to preserve the collected data?

- Where can your business find the data sources it needs?

Let's exemplify this context. Let's assume that your company owns a toothpaste brand and is part of a corporation in the personal care segment. It is very likely that it is a desire of the company to use Big Data technology to be able to understand the needs, buying habits and loyalty of customers.

From these requirements, it will be necessary to find data on customer sentiment and experience, while seeking data on how the customer views the competitive alternatives available in the market.

Some of this data will be available in traditional databases and systems, such as customer relationship management (CRM) systems and Data Warehouse.

But unfortunately, it is very likely that your company is looking to expand its analysis base beyond traditional data sources and will need to understand where to get these new data sources.

Obtaining the data is then the first job to be done. Here it is not only a question of knowing where to obtain the data, but also the form or type of the data as well as the quality and reliability of the data.

Good sources of sentiment data are found on social media, such as Facebook, Foursquare, Yelp, Pinterest, and Twitter. The fonts that will be selected can be determined by the habits of your customers.

For example, your ideal customer, the persona, may be very active on social media. However, your company can only operate in the business-to-business mode[3] of sales.

In this case, it is necessary to seriously analyze whether social media sites will contribute to the understanding of your customers more proactively. It will be necessary to find important B2B sites to be incorporated into Big Data analysis.

The problem is as big as the huge amount of data and the data sought is a grain of sand on the beach. The few snippets of messages that are information about customer sentiment toward the product are hidden in the vastness of the Internet. Additionally, the structure and types of this data vary from site to site, adding additional complexity and many costs. The company will need to understand the value of sifting through this data to gain supporting insights.

---

[3] Business to Business - B2B. It refers to the type of business done from business to business, rather than directly with the consumer. B2B companies are those that provide services to other companies, usually as outsourcers.

Some of these sources can be easily examined at a low cost, while others will require a more detailed ROI to determine the potential value of information about the company.

After identifying the sources and types of data, the company must then understand what can be done with the data. To do so, some questions about the data need to be asked:

- Can they be modified?

- Can they be stored locally for later use?

- Is there any limit on the amount of data that can be gathered in a given period?

- How often can the data be obtained?

- How often does the data change at the source?

The answers to these questions can help the company understand the economic impact of using Big Data and may raise new questions:

- What is the impact on the analysis of not having unrestricted access to a given source?

- How important is constant access?

- What will be the impact on revenue and product marketing decisions if a given data source is only accessed once each week?

The answers generate other questions until a satisfactory view of this scenario is obtained.

Understanding how often data is used by internal systems can help control costs.

If it is included in the requirements that it is necessary to analyze customer sentiment in real time, the cost to analyze time-related attributes will cause a significant increase in costs.

The cost generated only when you need to use the data is significantly lower and is more manageable.

Another factor in reducing costs is to consider whether the analysis may not be as fast or with less source data. The use of data and currency are the main factors of analysis of the Big Data economy.

Some data source vendors for Big Data charge to release ownership of your data, license it for specific use, or release it for non-destructive use. Others are more flexible, charging little or no access costs or excessive usage requirements.

The company, for example, will need to examine each source and ensure that proper care is taken regarding who owns the data and who owns the work products that use the data.

Some licensing data may limit usage for calculation and disposal. You can use the data as part of a process analysis, but you must then delete the data at the conclusion of the calculations.

Other vendors may allow you to use the data but require you to purge this data when your analysis and calculations are complete, returning the calculations and analyses to increase the value of the data source to other customers.

Great care must be taken to protect company information and work products as one integrates Big Data into their work environment.

In the previous example, it is possible that the company wants to include in the requirements that verify customer sentiment a certain period of time. To meet this new requirement, new questions will be generated:

- Has the customer changed their sentiment towards the brand in the last month? Six months? One year?

- How did the customer behave in relation to the competition's offers in the same periods?

Knowing how often a company needs to access data can help predict the costs associated with data capacity, accessibility, and currency.

Once you've decided on the approach that will best contribute to achieving your company's business objectives, you can begin to operate that approach. The ability to operate the approach you choose to leverage big data will allow your company to move to the steady state of economics, the state where costs are known and stabilized and data sources have proven reliable and useful.

However, over time, costs may change due to tariff and licensing corrections, and new issues may become important. However, your company will have the right foundation.

Continuing with the example, the company needs to understand how its processes will be affected. You need to decide whether to identify new customers and add them, as prospective customers, to customer databases.

In other cases, it will be necessary to create processes to understand how Big Data can be used to create understandings about your products or seek deeper understandings about customer loyalty and retention.

In any of these cases, it is important to model the costs required to change existing work processes. The true economic impact of Big Data will require balancing the costs of such changes with the potential benefit.

The next step in the implementation of Big Data is to understand the impact of the technology. It would be very nice to be able to continue to use a lot of existing technologies and applications in the company when Big Data is applied in the workflow.

However, it is more likely that new technologies will be needed to extract the maximum economic value from Big Data investments. As discussed earlier, many new and different tools are available for Big Data.

Existing technologies are too fragile because they were designed for a specific task or because they are too simplistic to solve the stress of large data applications.

In the example, the company's needs will create processes and technologies. Each of these requirements will drive the need for new skills and modernization of existing skills in many departments, but most visibly in the IT department and in the areas of business analysts.

All of the costs discussed earlier must be balanced against the potential outcomes of the investments. In the next phase, we need to analyze the ROI for Big Data.

3.4.2   Making something difficult easy.

Now that you have a better understanding of what you need to do to introduce Big Data into your company, think about how you can do it. Here are some tips to consider when bringing Big Data into your business:

Tip 1 – Hire those who already know.

- Don't object to hiring one or two experts as consultants.

- If they know the context of Big Data deployment well, they are able to mentor their teams.

Tip 2 – Hire good training.

- Take courses and read books on the subject.

- Do research on Big Data on the Internet.

- Participate in discussion groups.

- Attend industry conferences and events.

Tip 3 - Try it.

- Plan for failure. Rapid failure is becoming mandatory for contemporary technology-driven companies. The best lessons learned often come from failures.

- Study other people's experiences.

Tip 4 - Set appropriate expectations.

- Correctly set expectations can mean the difference between success and failure.

- A successful project can be seen as a failure if the business benefits are exaggerated or if it takes 50% longer to deliver.

- Big data offers enormous potential, but only if costs and time for its implementation are calculated correctly.

Tip 5 - Be holistic.

- Try looking at all dimensions for any Big Data initiative.

- If the project is delivered on time and on budget, but the end users are not trained or ready to use it, the project can result in failure.

- The most successful project managers understand that good

results need to be thought of as a whole that includes people, processes, and technology.

4   Big Data for Small Business.

There is no doubt that Big Data is one of the major trends for the most diverse sectors of the market in the coming years. A survey by Gartner shows that, by 2030, three out of four companies intend to invest in Big Data in their business. But is it possible to develop Big Data solutions for small businesses as well?

Over time, since the concept of Big Data began to become better known, starting in 2008, the idea was created that this tool would only be possible to be applied in large companies. After all, they are able to afford costs, create departments focused on the topic and structure ways to monitor large volumes of data.

But this is not true. More and more small businesses have been using Big Data to help solve issues that are important in their daily lives. Every day 2.5 billion bytes of information are generated on the internet. And in this number everything fits — the post on the social network, the report of a bank transaction, a GIF sent by a messaging app, a heart *emoji*.

There are millions of possibilities and that doesn't mean you should look at all of them. It would be impossible and a great waste of time (Kamioka et al., 2014).

However, several tools can be useful to analyze a large volume of information that is really useful for your business. To do this, the first step is to know exactly what you want with Big Data.

See this and other tips below.

1. Have a goal with Big Data.

    First of all, using Big Data for small businesses must start from a concrete objective. Where do you want to go with the analysis of a certain volume of data? Answering this question is crucial for the development of your business from Big Data.

    If your goal is to invest in user experience, for example, it is important to filter the data that is generated on social networks, such as comments, photos, stories, reviews on sales sites, recommendations, among others.

    From an analysis of the raw information collected in the most diverse channels, it is possible to identify the actions that should be implemented in order to increase engagement with these people.

    If your focus at this moment is to build customer loyalty and ensure future sales from those who already know you, filter the information obtained through forms, sales data, comments on social networks to develop strategies for the future.

2. Know your customer's habits.

    Large supermarket or pharmacy companies know very well who their customers are and try, in any way, to standardize behaviors with the sole purpose of increasing sales.

    Don't be surprised if one day you enter an establishment and come across the diaper shelf next to the beer shelf on a Friday night.

    It is very difficult for this to be just a coincidence. In fact, it is the analysis of thousands of purchases over time through Big Data tools and cross-referencing several different types of data. It's like putting on paper a purchase profile of your average customer.

In the case of a small company, the logic can also be adopted. Big Data for small businesses can help you find consumption patterns that can translate into increased sales.

3. Keep an eye on the metrics.

Another way to use Big Data for small businesses is to focus on metrics in the online environment.

Crossing sales data from e-commerce platforms with sponsored campaigns on Facebook, for example, can help define the best time for ad scheduling or the type of audience that has to receive these posts. The tip is to analyze the data and test.

4. Do not despise information.

Although it is not recommended that a small business wants to "embrace the world" from Big Data, it is also recommended not to disregard information that is generated in sales and can be easily collected.

It may be that, at first glance, you don't see anything wrong with knowing the neighborhood where your customer lives. However, it is precisely this information that can make the difference when designing a campaign.

Try to check for trends hidden within data volumes. Deciphering these "stories" behind the raw reports can mean the leap you need to amplify your performance in a particular location or segment.

5. Always inform yourself.

The Big Data market is constantly changing. Every day we are faced with the discovery of new tools and ways of seeing and analyzing the data generated by various sources. It is important to stay up to date on industry news and keep an open mind to innovate whenever necessary.

Several experts have treated information as the main strategic asset of companies in the 21st century. And they are not wrong. The important thing is to know what information is necessary and desirable, how to get to it and how to analyze it. It's a good challenge.

4.1   3 Big Data tools for small businesses.

Big Data tools can be used by virtually any business. The important thing is to know the available technology and be aware of the desired results.

Technology opens up possibilities for small and medium-sized entrepreneurs. Entrepreneurs can also benefit from technology to plan the future of the company.

In the last ten years, small and medium-sized companies have gained a competitive advantage, as they now have access to information with the same agility as large companies, without the need for large investments.

Part of the solutions can, in fact, be free for the company. There are free, open-source public databases and cross-referencing systems that can be customized as needed.

Special labor and necessary infrastructure, however, are not cheap. Therefore, it may not pay for a small company to hire a specialized professional, but it is always possible to hire a consultancy.

Here are 3 recommended tools at low or no cost that can be used by small and medium-sized businesses:

1. Google Analytics.

    Google's free tool has interesting solutions with features that can be used by small businesses.

The main objective of Google Analytics is not only to know how many users access a website, but how these users behave when browsing the various pages and sections of this website.

It is based on the information collected that it is possible to analyze whether visitors have the expected behavior in response to a certain online marketing campaign.

Traffic monitoring is one of the main functions of any online activity and indispensable for business management in this segment, and Google Analytics, or GA as it is also known, is the standard tool on the market.

2. ClearStory Data.

ClearStory Data is a scalable, cloud-based business intelligence solution that enables businesses, organizations, and departments to uncover business insights and collaborate on them.

The solution combines data from disparate sources and generates actionable, interactive insights that users can explore. It is used in various industries that include manufacturing, retail, media and entertainment, financial services, consumer packaged goods or CPG, food and beverage, healthcare, and life sciences.

Its primary function is to analyze customers, marketing data, operational efficiency, and sales performance for database preparation through its inference and profiling engine, which eliminates the normally time-consuming process of capturing and organizing data for analysis.

To speed up data exploration and interpretation, the solution uses interactive visualizations that allow new questions to be asked for the evolution of analyses and conclusions.

3. IBM Watson Analytics.

The Watson platform is the combination of Artificial Intelligence technology and human language for analyzing huge amounts of data and obtaining answers quickly.

In the age of digitized information, it is common for exorbitant amounts of information to be generated in the cloud every day, such as posts, photos, formulas, searches, texts, and more. In most cases, this is unstructured data and, therefore, is not visible to technology and computers.

And this is where IBM's Watson comes in. As it is a system based on cognitive computing, it is able to interpret this data, learn from it and create lines of reasoning from it. It is through this concept that several industries are reinventing themselves with the use of Watson, such as retail, banking, health and the travel sector, for example.

This IBM product can be easily used even in a small business. With it, the manager has access to advanced business analysis without having knowledge about technical aspects such as data mining, for example.

4.2   18 Tips to maximize customer relationships.

Big Data analytics have the potential to improve various processes in companies. As many of the efforts are directed to making decisions about strategies and planning to strengthen the relationship with customers, it is important to be aware of these tips.

1º. Predict what customers want.

It is possible to predict what your customers want and always be one step ahead. Yes, this is possible through Big Data actions. There are tools that analyze data related to user behavior on your website, for example.

The so-called heat map demonstrates the pages or areas of a website that are most accessed by customers. In this way, if many people access a page of a particular product in an e-commerce, for example, it means that it is something very searched and that arouses the desire of these people. How about, then, creating a promotion to sell many units of this item? This is using Big Data to anticipate the needs of your customers.

So far, we've talked a lot about customers, but they're not the only people your company can act more accurately with data management.

2nd. Guide salespeople and the accounting department to visualize data in real time.

The orders placed by salespeople can always be viewed in real time by the entire company team, when using appropriate management software. This makes the write-offs in stock be done correctly.

The other sellers, following this data, will know when a product is no longer in stock and can no longer be sold, for example. The accounting sector, in turn, will have a projection of the amounts that will enter into the company's cash.

3rd. Use data to lower operational costs.

If your company notices that customers are no longer interested in a certain type of product, which has had a drop in sales, for example, it is possible to suspend the production of that item.

The idea is that operating costs are reduced and that there are no expenses with the production and storage of products that no longer bring the financial return expected by the company.

4th. Insert Big Data into customer relationship management.

Big Data plays a key role in customer relationship management. By analyzing large volumes of data, businesses can gain valuable insights into customer behavior, preferences, and needs, allowing for a personalized and targeted approach.

One of the main applications of Big Data in customer relationship management is the personalization of experiences. Based on real-time and historical data, businesses can tailor their offerings, communications, and marketing strategies according to each customer's individual preferences. This creates a more relevant and personalized experience, increasing customer satisfaction and loyalty.

In addition to personalization, Big Data can also be used to identify trends and patterns of customer behavior. Data analysis allows you to identify which products, services, or promotions are most attractive to certain customer segments, helping in strategic decision-making. With this information, businesses can optimize their marketing campaigns and initiatives, directing efforts and resources to the most promising areas.

Another important aspect is the proactive detection of customer problems or dissatisfaction. With real-time data analysis, it is possible to quickly identify negative trends, such as recurring complaints, quality issues, or service failures. This early detection allows companies to take corrective action in an agile way, solving problems before they become more serious and affect the company's image.

In addition, Big Data allows for a better understanding of the customer's lifestyle. By analyzing data about the customer journey, from the first contact to loyalty, companies can identify critical points and opportunities for improvement at each stage of the process. This makes it possible to adopt more effective strategies to attract, convert and retain customers, maximizing the value of the relationship with each one of them.

5th. Ensure good communication through various channels.

Contacts with customers, for certain strategies, such as follow-up or after-sales, for example, can be made through various means of communication. Email, telephones, social networks, and even correspondence written and sent by mail, if your audience profile likes this media, can be used.

However, for these communications to be made with quality and accuracy, it is necessary to have a solid base with all the addresses of your customers. This is only possible with good Big Data management, in which data is always stored and updated frequently.

6th. Analyze your customers' payment preferences.

When a customer makes a purchase, through an e-commerce or even in person at a store, he needs to choose a payment method. Thus, if it is noticed that a certain customer prefers to pay with cash instead of credit card, the company can create exclusive and targeted offers for him.

If it is possible to grant discounts to those who pay in cash and inform these customers of this, the company will certainly have an increase in sales during this period.

7th. Use data to build personas.

The concept of target audience is already somewhat outdated for companies, because, currently, the same company can serve several market niches within a large group. Thus, a women's clothing store can cater to both more conservative ladies, and with a classic look, as well as young people who like to adopt a bolder look, for example.

The ways of approaching these two groups of people cannot be the same, do you agree? Therefore, classifying a target audience only as "women" may not be enough in relationship strategies.

Personas are semi-fictional characters that represent the different customer profiles that a company may have. Within this context, the data collected by Big Data tools can contribute to the construction of these characters and the communication with your customers to be more efficient.

8th. Get to know customers to drive more sales.

When a sale is successfully completed, it is essential for the salesperson to take the opportunity to collect the customer's data. This valuable information can later be utilized in future negotiations, paving the way for additional sales. However, it is not only about collecting this data but also using it strategically to better understand the behavior of buyers.

By carefully analyzing customer data, it is possible to gain valuable insights into their spending habits, preferences, and needs. This in-depth understanding provides a solid foundation for making targeted and personalized approaches, increasing sales effectiveness.

For example, if a specific customer has shown interest in sports-related products in their previous purchase, the salesperson can utilize that information when making a new approach. By recommending products or services that are aligned with the customer's interests, the chances of successful sales increase significantly.

In addition, knowing customers also allows you to identify cross-selling or upselling opportunities. By analyzing buying patterns and complementary products, it is possible to offer the customer related products that can add value to their shopping experience. This not only increases the average value of transactions but also strengthens customer relationships.

In the financial industry, every sales opportunity is valuable. So, make the most of customer data to understand their needs, anticipate their demands, and offer customized solutions. This proactive and targeted approach will result in an increase in profits and business growth.

Remember that the collection of customer data must be done in accordance with the applicable privacy and data protection laws. It is essential to ensure the security and confidentiality of customers' personal information, respecting their privacy and obtaining appropriate consent for the use of their data.

9th. Use data to address customer dissatisfaction.

It is already a common practice in modern society to share frustrations on social networks. Thus, when a customer is not well served in a commercial establishment or buys a product that he does not like, he can use social networks, such as Facebook and Twitter, as well as complaint sites, such as Reclame Aqui, to vent about his dissatisfaction.

The content of these complaints can also be stored, and the information cross-checked. This cross-referencing can identify the main reasons for complaints that customers make on the Internet, allowing possible mistakes made by the company, with regard to the relationship with customers, to be corrected and avoided.

10th. Employing Big Data in competitor observation.

In the competitive world of business, it is essential to closely monitor the actions and strategies of competitors. Big Data offers a unique opportunity to collect, analyze, and extract relevant information from large data sets, allowing for detailed observation of the competition.

One of the main advantages of using Big Data in observing the competition is the ability to identify market trends and patterns.

By analyzing large volumes of data, it is possible to gain insights into the strategies that are working for competitors, as well as those that are not bringing desirable results. This allows you to adjust your own strategy, based on concrete evidence and up-to-date information.

In addition, Big Data can reveal detailed information about competitors' customer behavior. By analyzing data from social networks, transaction records, online searches, and other sources, it is possible to better understand the profile of the competitor's target audience, their preferences, needs, and expectations. This information can be used to fine-tune your own value proposition and differentiate yourself in the market.

Another benefit of Big Data in observing the competition is the ability to anticipate strategic moves. By analyzing indicators, such as price, product offerings, marketing campaigns, and other aspects of competitors' business, you can identify potential opportunities or threats that could affect your own business. This allows you to make more informed decisions and react quickly to market changes.

However, it is important to note that Big Data analysis requires technical expertise and appropriate tools. To obtain accurate and relevant results, it is necessary to have a robust data collection, storage, and analysis system, as well as qualified professionals to interpret the results and extract meaningful insights.

11th.   Analyze the ROI of digital marketing strategies.

Digital marketing is on the rise and, increasingly, companies use new media to generate leads, that is, to arouse interest in people who can become their customers.

This, however, must be done through an investment. And to know if such a cost generated positive results, it is necessary to calculate the Return on Investment – ROI.

Big Data can help in this regard, since it is easier to mine conversion data and thus generate the numbers that should be applied to the ROI formula.

12th. Look for more data sources for marketing actions.

As discussed earlier, Big Data contributes to the construction of personas, that is, so that the company can more easily recognize its ideal audience niche. This is also important in marketing actions, since advertising and advertising actions can be more targeted.

For this, professionals in the sector will be able to search for data so that the actions have more results.

In addition, through Big Data tools, it is possible to install automatic data collectors, such as observing the "traces" that customers leave when they access your company's website or blog, for example.

13º. Study your competitors' performance.

It is obvious that your competitors will not make confidential company information public, such as financial reports, for example. However, there is some data that can be easily analyzed, such as interactions on social networks.

If you notice that your competitor ran a marketing campaign on Facebook and got few likes, reactions, and comments on the post, for example, it means that it was not successful. This is important so that you don't do anything similar and analyze what they did wrong.

14º. Practice benchmarking.

Benchmarking or mystery shopping actions are used to "extract" information from your competitors. To do this, someone from your company can contact the competition, posing as a customer and, thus, get interesting information, such as prices and payment and delivery conditions, for example.

All this data needs to be correctly recorded and then analyzed so that it can be compared with the company's reality and develop strategies that make the business a more attractive option for customers.

15th. Analyze the behavior of competitors.

It is also important to analyze the behavior of competitors on social networks and other media, such as in ads made on television or radio. This is important to understand how the competitor's brand positioning generates results for the public, so that it is possible to develop their own identity.

The crossover of interactions that your competitors' customers make on social media is also relevant. This is because by identifying the failures made by these companies, it is possible for your company to act strategically so that customers see your business as a better option in this segment.

16º. Do A/B testing.

A/B tests are comparisons between variables that can be used to obtain better results in decision-making. If you have an e-commerce, for example, you can vary the positioning of the products on the website, as well as the colors of the shopping button.

In this way, if you sometimes use a green button, sometimes red, and detect that one of the colors generates more clicks than the other, you can leave the one that presents more results as definitive.

But how to measure the data from this test? It's simple: through a Big Data tool that records the actions that people take on your page.

17th. Practice the pyramid of knowledge technique.

The concept of the Pyramid of Knowledge, also called the DIKW Hierarchy, is very relevant for those who seek to develop organized work with good results. Basically, it is a hierarchical system in which there are four pillars: Data, Information, Knowledge and Wisdom.

Adapted from the concept of the pyramid proposed by Abraham H. Maslow in the 1950s, the pyramid of knowledge is a technique that is based on the assumption that the data collected by Big Data tools contributes to decisions being made more assertively and wisely.

The process begins by preparing a question that demonstrates a problem that needs to be solved by the company. From this question, we go through the blocks of the pyramid as follows.

Block 1 – Data collection.

Data is qualitative, categorical information. In this block occurs the essential difference between this pyramid and the traditional pyramids of knowledge. Here it is necessary to have Big Data as an objective and collect data from texts, photos, numbers, among other types of data collected that will be complemented with structured databases.

Block 2 – Information.

We can summarize what information is by considering that information is data endowed with relevance and purpose. It has meaning and is organized by some purpose in the company.

In this block, the data collected must be transformed into information, that is, it needs to be interpreted in order to discover what meaning it has.

Block 3 – Knowledge

This is the block in which the Information is used. Knowledge refers to the ability to create a model that describes the object and indicates the actions to be implemented, the decisions to be made.

Based on knowledge, it should be possible to use the information so that decisions can be made with an informed basis. The problem raised in the step of the question must be solved in the best possible way.

Block 4 – Wisdom

Once the problem has been solved, the data can also contribute to the company acting wisely and thus knowing what the best initiatives for the future are. This means that Big Data can contribute to problems not arising again on other occasions.

18th.   Analyze data in real time.

Through Big Data, it is possible to monitor your company's data in real time, and this is important for decision-making. The objective of this monitoring is that all the company's decisions are made with a basis.

Not only the big decisions, such as whether or not to make an investment that involves a lot of money, but even simple day-today tasks, such as contacting a customer, can be supported by data.

One of the areas of companies that benefits the most from Big Data is marketing, as all decisions made in this sector must be very important.

5   Cost Analysis in Different Cloud Models.

Cloud computing has emerged as one of the fundamental pillars of Big Data infrastructure, redefining not only how data is stored and processed, but also how costs are distributed and managed. However, the apparent simplicity of the cloud hides a web of economic complexities that demand deep and critical analysis.

5.1   The Triangulation of Cloud Models: Public, Private, and Hybrid.

The choice between public, private, and hybrid cloud is not merely technical; It's a strategic decision that reverberates through every layer of the organization, from infrastructure to data governance. Each model carries with it a unique set of costs and benefits, which must be carefully weighed.

5.1.1   Public Cloud: The Illusion of Cost-Free Scalability.

The public cloud, offered by giants such as Amazon Web Services (AWS), Microsoft Azure, and Google Cloud, is often celebrated for its scalability and pay-as-you-go pricing model. However, this apparent flexibility hides a number of hidden costs.

First, there's the cost of latency: in high-demand environments, performance can be compromised, especially when multiple users compete for the same resources.

Second, security costs, while mitigated by providers, still require significant investments in encryption, firewalls, and continuous monitoring. Third, the cost of compliance: In highly regulated industries such as healthcare and finance, the public cloud may require costly adaptations to meet regulations such as GDPR and HIPAA.

5.1.2   Private Cloud: The Price of Exclusivity.

The private cloud, on the other hand, gives you complete control over the infrastructure, but at a considerable cost. Acquiring hardware, maintaining data centers, and needing specialized teams represent initial and ongoing investments that can be prohibitive for many organizations. Additionally, scalability is limited by the physical capacity of the data center, which can lead to additional costs in fast-growing scenarios.

However, for organizations that handle highly sensitive data or that operate in strict regulatory environments, the private cloud can justify its high costs through increased security and control.

5.1.3   Hybrid Cloud: The Precarious Balance

Hybrid cloud emerges as an attempt to balance the benefits of public and private cloud, but this approach is not without its challenges.

Integration between public and private environments requires middleware solutions, orchestration tools, and specialized technical expertise, all of which come with significant costs. In addition, managing data distributed across multiple clouds can lead to operational inefficiencies and unforeseen costs, especially when there is a need for constant synchronization between environments.

5.2   Data Transfer Between Clouds: The Invisible Cost of Interoperability.

One of the most overlooked aspects of Big Data costing is the transfer of data between different cloud providers. While data portability is a fundamental principle of cloud computing, the reality is that moving large volumes of data between AWS, Google Cloud, Azure, and other providers can incur substantial costs.

5.2.1   Egress Costs: The Financial Trap.

Egress costs—charged when data moves from one cloud to another or to the internet—are often underestimated. Providers such as AWS and Azure charge significant fees per gigabyte transferred, which can result in exorbitant costs for organizations that rely on multiple clouds. For example, transferring 1 petabyte of data from AWS to another cloud can cost tens of thousands of dollars, depending on the region and destination provider.

5.2.2   Strategies to Minimize Transfer Costs.

To mitigate these costs, organizations can adopt several strategies. One of them is the use of direct connections (Direct Connect, in the case of AWS), which reduces egress costs by avoiding the public internet. Another approach is to consolidate data into a single cloud whenever possible, reducing the need for frequent transfers. In addition, compressing and deduplicating data prior to transfer can reduce data volume and, consequently, costs.

5.3   Trade-offs between Cost, Security, and Performance: An Inevitable Trilemma.

Choosing a cloud model inevitably involves trade-offs between cost, security, and performance. The public cloud can offer lower costs and greater scalability, but at the expense of reduced control over security and performance. Private clouds, on the other hand, offers increased security and predictable performance, but at a significantly higher financial cost. Hybrid cloud attempts to balance these trade-offs, but introduces additional complexities that can result in unforeseen costs.

5.3.1   Cost vs. Security: The Dilemma of Trust.

Security is one of the main factors that influence the choice of cloud model. While the public cloud relies on shared security measures, the private cloud allows for complete control over security and access policies. However, this control comes with a price: the need to invest in firewalls, intrusion detection systems, and specialized security teams.

Hybrid cloud, on the other hand, requires careful management of security policies between public and private environments, which can increase complexity and costs.

5.3.2 Cost vs. Performance: The Quest for Efficiency.

Performance is another critical factor. The public cloud can suffer from latency issues and competition for resources, especially at peak times. Private cloud, on the other hand, offers predictable performance but at a high infrastructure cost. Hybrid cloud tries to balance these aspects, but integration between environments can introduce latency and inefficiencies that impact overall performance.

5.4 The Future of Cloud Costs: Emerging Trends and Challenges.

As cloud computing continues to evolve, new challenges and trends emerge, each with significant implications for Big Data costs. The growing adoption of edge computing, for example, promises to reduce data transfer costs by processing information closer to the source, but requires investments in distributed infrastructure. Similarly, the rise of technologies such as Kubernetes and serverless computing offers new opportunities to optimize costs, but it also introduces complexities that can result in unforeseen costs.

6 Data Deactivation and Disposal Costs.

In the age of Big Data, where the accumulation of information is often seen as a strategic asset, the disposal and deactivation of data emerges as a paradox. On the one hand, excessive data retention can lead to unsustainable storage costs and security risks; on the other hand, improper disposal can result in privacy violations, regulatory fines, and reputational damage.

6.1 Secure Data Disposal: An Ethical and Economic Imperative.

Secure data disposal is not only a technical issue, but also an ethical and economic one. In a world where data privacy and security are increasingly valued, organizations must address the costs associated with properly disposing of sensitive and obsolete information.

6.1.1 Direct Costs of Safe Disposal.

The process of secure data disposal involves a number of direct costs:

- Cost of the technology required to ensure irreversible destruction of data. This includes the use of overwriting software, which replaces existing data with random information, and the physical destruction of storage devices such as hard drives and SSDs.

- Cost of certification, where third-party organizations are hired to ensure that disposal has been carried out in accordance with international standards, such as ISO/IEC 27040. Third, there is the cost of documentation, which involves creating and maintaining detailed records of the disposal process, which are essential for audits and regulatory compliance.

6.1.2 Indirect Costs and Associated Risks.

In addition to direct costs, safe data disposal also involves indirect costs and risks. One of them is the risk of incomplete disposal, where

sensitive data can be recovered by malicious third parties, resulting in privacy violations and regulatory fines.

Another indirect cost is the impact on the organization's reputation, where failures to dispose of data can lead to a loss of trust on the part of customers and partners. In addition, there is the cost of lost opportunity, where excessive retention of stale data can consume resources that could be allocated to more strategic initiatives.

6.2   Infrastructure Decommissioning: The Cost of Technological Transition.

Decommissioning aging infrastructure is another critical aspect of Big Data costs. As technologies evolve, organizations are forced to migrate to new solutions, which involves shutting down old systems and transitioning to more modern and efficient environments.

6.2.1 Decommissioning Costs.

Decommissioning obsolete infrastructure involves a number of costs:

- Cost of assessment, where the organization must determine which systems and equipment need to be decommissioned and which can be reused or recycled.

- Cost of data migration, where critical information must be transferred from old systems to new ones, a process that can be complex and costly. Third, there is the cost of the physical destruction of equipment, which must be carried out in a safe and environmentally responsible manner, often involving the hiring of companies that specialize in electronics recycling.

6.2.2 Compliance Costs and Environmental Risks.

Infrastructure decommissioning also involves compliance costs and environmental risks. Organizations must ensure that the disposal of electronic equipment is carried out in accordance with environmental standards, such as the RoHS (Restriction of Hazardous Substances) Directive in the European Union.

Failure to comply with these standards can result in significant fines and penalties. Additionally, there is the environmental risk associated with improper disposal of electronic equipment, which can lead to soil and water contamination, resulting in cleanup costs and reputational damage.

6.3 Strategies to Minimize Disposal and Decommissioning Costs.

Given the complexity and costs associated with secure data disposal and infrastructure decommissioning, organizations must adopt strategies to minimize these costs.

6.3.1 Data Retention Policies.

One of the most effective strategies is the implementation of clear and well-defined data retention policies. These policies should establish deadlines for the retention of different types of data, ensuring that obsolete information is disposed of in a secure and timely manner.

Additionally, retention policies should be reviewed regularly to ensure that they align with the needs of the organization and current regulations.

6.3.2   Automated Disposal Technologies.

Another strategy is the use of automated disposal technologies, which can reduce the costs and risks associated with manual data disposal. These technologies include automated overwriting software and systems for the physical destruction of storage devices, which can be programmed to perform disposal safely and efficiently.

6.3.3   Partnerships with Experts.

Finally, organizations can minimize disposal and decommissioning costs by partnering with experts in secure data disposal and electronic equipment recycling. These partnerships can ensure that disposal is carried out in accordance with best practices and international standards, reducing the risks of privacy violations and environmental damage.

7   Pitfalls to Avoid Better Big Data Management.

Big data management has become increasingly important for companies in all industries, as the amount of data generated and available today is exponential. However, care must be taken to avoid falling into traps that may compromise the efficiency of this management and, consequently, the results obtained. In this text, I will address some of these pitfalls and provide tips to avoid them.

The lack of proper planning is a common pitfall in big data management and can significantly compromise the results obtained by companies. Many organizations are drawn to the promise of insights and competitive advantages that big data management can offer and end up diving into data collection without a clear strategy in mind.

Setting objectives and goals is essential for the success of big data management. Without a clear direction, companies can end up collecting unnecessary data or getting lost in the vastness of information available. It is crucial to identify the purpose of big data management and how it aligns with the organization's strategic objectives. This could include increasing operational efficiency, enhancing customer experience, identifying market opportunities, or improving decision-making.

In addition to setting objectives, it is important to set success metrics to measure the impact of big data management. These metrics can vary according to the objectives set, and may include indicators such as increased revenue, cost reduction, improved customer satisfaction, or efficiency in data processing. Having clear metrics allows the company to track its progress and assess whether it is achieving the desired results.

Another pitfall related to lack of planning is the lack of an adequate structure for collecting and storing data. Big data management involves dealing with large volumes of information coming from a variety of sources. Without proper structure, data can become disorganized, making it difficult to analyze and gain relevant insights. It is necessary to define a data collection system that is efficient and consistent, ensuring the integrity and quality of the data from the moment it is captured.

In addition, it is essential to have a proper storage and management system for the data collected. Choosing a scalable and secure storage infrastructure is critical to handling the massive amount of data generated in the context of big data.

The lack of a robust storage structure can lead to problems such as data loss, poor performance, and difficulties in data analysis. It is important to invest in suitable storage technologies and solutions, such as NoSQL databases, data warehouses, or cloud storage services, that can handle the scalability and variety of data.

In addition to proper planning for data collection and storage, it is equally important to consider data governance. Many companies face the challenge of dealing with unstructured, inconsistent, and outdated data.

The lack of proper governance can lead to problems such as data duplication, lack of standardization, and difficulties in identifying data sources. It is critical to establish policies and processes to ensure the quality, integrity, and security of data throughout its lifespan. This includes defining responsibilities, implementing data cleansing and enrichment practices, standardizing formats, and adopting metadata management techniques.

Another common pitfall is the overestimation of the quantity of data at the expense of quality. Often, companies focus on collecting as much data as possible but neglect the importance of the relevance and quality of that data. The focus should be on getting the right data that is relevant to the needs of the business. Not all data is equally useful or representative, and analyzing irrelevant or low-quality data can lead to inaccurate results and mistaken conclusions. It is necessary to define clear criteria for the selection and evaluation of data, considering their origin, reliability, and relevance to the analyses.

Another pitfall to avoid is the lack of proper control and monitoring of data usage. Big data management involves dealing with sensitive information, such as personal customer data, financial or strategic company information. It is essential to implement robust security measures to protect this data from unauthorized access, privacy breaches, and cyberattacks.

In addition, it is important to have control over who has access to the data and how it is used. Lack of proper control and monitoring can lead to data misuse, violation of data protection regulations, and legal and reputational consequences for the company. It is recommended to implement data access and use policies, defining access permissions based on the responsibilities and needs of users, in addition to conducting regular audits to ensure compliance and identify any irregularities.

It is essential to establish the purpose of the use of the data, identify the relevant information to be collected, and determine the metrics that will be used to evaluate the success of the management. Without strategic planning, it is easy to get lost in the immensity of data and not get the desired results.

Another common pitfall is underestimating the importance of data quality. Massive information collection can be overwhelming, but if the data is inaccurate, incomplete, or outdated, all the management effort will be in vain. It is essential to invest time and resources in verifying and cleaning data, ensuring its quality before it is used for analysis and decision-making. Additionally, it is important to establish continuous monitoring processes to ensure that the data remains reliable over time.

One pitfall related to data quality is the lack of integration between different sources of information. Often, companies deal with data from several different sources, such as internal systems, social networks, market analysis sites, among others. For efficient big data management, it is necessary to integrate these different data sources, ensuring their coherence and providing a complete view of the available information. Lack of integration can lead to incomplete analyses and erroneous conclusions.

Another pitfall to avoid is the lack of adequate resources for big data management. Processing, storing, and analyzing large volumes of data requires robust infrastructure and efficient systems. It is necessary to invest in appropriate equipment, technologies, and software solutions to handle the complexity and volume of data. In addition, it is also important to have trained and experienced professionals, such as data scientists and big data engineers, to ensure the correct use and interpretation of data.

Lack of data security is another common pitfall. Big data management involves dealing with sensitive and confidential information, which requires the implementation of robust security measures. This includes the use of encryption, proper access control, monitoring for suspicious activity, and regular backups of the data. A security breach can compromise data integrity, customer privacy, and company reputation, making data protection a top priority.

Similarly, the lack of proper governance can also become a trap. It is essential to establish clear policies, guidelines, and processes for the use, access, and sharing of data. This includes defining responsibilities, limiting access to sensitive information, and establishing procedures for the deletion and retention of data. The absence of governance can lead to decisions based on inconsistent data, lack of compliance with regulations, and even lawsuits.

Finally, it is important to highlight the trap of sticking only to technology. While implementing proper technologies is essential for efficient big data management, the human aspect cannot be neglected.

The success of big data management depends on both the technology and the people involved. It is necessary to train and educate teams to correctly use data, interpret analyses, and make evidence-based decisions. Cross-functional collaboration and effective communication also play a crucial role in big data management.

Thus, to avoid the pitfalls in big data management, it is essential to:

1. Conduct strategic planning: Set clear objectives, identify relevant information, and define successful metrics.

2. Ensure data quality: Invest in verifying, cleaning, and monitoring data to ensure its accuracy and reliability.

3. Integrate different sources of information: Integrate data from multiple sources to get a complete and coherent view of the information available.

4. Have adequate resources: Invest in infrastructure, technologies, and trained professionals to deal with the challenges of big data management.

5. Prioritize data security: Implement robust security measures to protect sensitive and confidential information.

6. Establish proper governance: Define clear policies, guidelines, and processes for the use, access, and sharing of data.

7. Value the human aspect: Empower teams, foster collaboration, and communicate efficiently to ensure effective use of data.

By being aware of these pitfalls and adopting appropriate practices, businesses will be better prepared to derive maximum value and benefits from big data management. It is worth mentioning that the big data landscape is constantly evolving, and it is important to be up-to-date on new technologies and approaches to ensure increasingly efficient results.

8 Technological Trends and Cost Optimization in Big Data.

The Big Data market is constantly evolving, and technological trends play a crucial role in cost optimization. With the increasing complexity of data environments, the search for more accessible, flexible, and efficient solutions is a strategic goal for companies. Below, the main trends and their implications for infrastructure and operating costs are detailed:

8.1 Cloud Computing: Cost Reduction and Scalability.

Cloud computing remains one of the top alternatives for businesses looking to reduce upfront costs in Big Data. Providers such as AWS (Amazon Web Services), Microsoft Azure, and Google Cloud offer pay-as-you-go payment models, eliminating the need for large upfront investments in hardware.

Financial Advantages:

- Avoids costs of acquiring, maintaining, and upgrading physical equipment.

- It offers instant scalability, allowing you to adjust resources as demand.

- On-demand and subscription plans can reduce operating costs by up to 30%.

Cost Examples:

- Storage: $0.023 per GB-month (AWS S3 - Standard).

- Processing: Cloud compute instances range from $0.01 to $2 per hour, depending on the configuration.

- Data Transfer: Some regions offer free outbound traffic up to a limit, reducing costs.

Companies that adopt 100% cloud solutions gain access to cutting-edge technologies, such as managed data lakes, real-time analytics, and integration of AI tools, without the need for physical infrastructure.

8.2   Hybrid Technologies: Flexibility and Customization.

Combining on-premises infrastructure with cloud services – a hybrid model – has become a common practice to balance costs and meet specific security and performance requirements.

Advantages of Hybrid Infrastructure:

- Latency Reduction: Sensitive or highly critical data can be processed locally, while the cloud is used for large-scale storage or analytics.

- Optimized Costs: The workload can be distributed efficiently, avoiding excessive costs in the public cloud for ongoing operations.

- Compliance and Regulation: Ensuring compliance with local regulations by storing critical data within the company.

Practical Scenarios:

- A company can store large volumes of historical data in the cloud (at a lower cost), while keeping data in active use on on-premises servers for immediate processing.

- Hybrid models are used to implement microservices architectures, integrating various solutions and optimizing resource allocation.

8.3   Automation and Artificial Intelligence: Efficiency and Waste Reduction.

Automation and artificial intelligence (AI) have transformed the way businesses manage their Big Data infrastructures. These technologies enable the most efficient use of available resources, while reducing costs associated with manual management and wasted capacity.

Resource Automation:

- Auto-scaling: Cloud platforms can automatically adjust allocated resources based on spikes in demand, avoiding idle capacity costs.

- Cost Optimization: Tools such as AWS Cost Explorer, Azure Cost Management, and Google Cloud Pricing Calculator allow you to monitor and adjust resource usage.

Applied Artificial Intelligence:

- Demand Forecasting: AI models are used to predict workloads by optimizing cluster and storage allocation.

- Intelligent Data Management: AI-powered solutions prioritize relevant data for analysis and discard redundant or unnecessary information.

- Reduction of Operating Costs: Automation reduces the dependence on intensive human labor in administrative tasks, reducing expenses with specialized labor.

Implementation Examples:

- Databricks and Cloudera integrate AI for real-time monitoring and tuning of data infrastructure.

- Machine Learning Ops (MLOps) tools automate the lifecycle of AI models, optimizing long-term costs.

8.4   A conclusion.

By combining strategies such as cloud computing, hybrid technologies, and AI-based automation, companies are able to not only reduce upfront costs but also improve operational efficiency over time. These trends represent the future of Big Data management, enabling organizations to compete in an increasingly data-driven marketplace while optimizing the return on their technology investments.

9   Conclusion.

Throughout this book, we have explored the complexities of the costs involved in adopting and managing Big Data, demystifying its financial pitfalls and presenting effective strategies for optimizing investments. From the initial infrastructure to the challenges of data security and governance, to the hidden costs and impact of cloud computing models, each chapter has provided valuable insights for businesses and professionals to make informed and strategic decisions.

Understanding and managing the costs of Big Data is not just a matter of reducing expenses, but of maximizing the value of data as a competitive asset. By adopting best practices and utilizing automation and artificial intelligence tools, organizations can balance operational efficiency and innovation without compromising their budgets. As we have discussed, cost optimization is not an isolated event, but an ongoing process that requires constant adaptation and monitoring in the face of rapid technological changes.

However, this book is only one piece of the puzzle. Big Data is one of the many fundamental pillars of the artificial intelligence revolution, and understanding its financial impact is just the beginning. For a more comprehensive and in-depth view, we invite you to explore the other books in the Big Data and Artificial Intelligence collection, where we address the other essential components that shape this digital transformation: from modeling and machine learning to AI ethics and regulation.

Each volume of the collection is designed to offer structured and applied knowledge, helping professionals and companies navigate the vast and dynamic universe of artificial intelligence. If you want to continue this journey and improve your skills, our collection is your next essential read.

The future of business and technology belongs to those who know how to decipher and harness the power of data. By reading the other titles, you will be prepared to turn challenges into opportunities and lead in the information age.

Invest in your knowledge. Keep exploring, learning, and innovating.

10 Bibliography.

ACQUISTI, A., TAYLOR, C., & WAGMAN, L. (2016). The economics of privacy. Journal of Economic Literature, 54(2), 442-92.

AMAZON WEB SERVICES. (2023). AWS Pricing Calculator. Available at: **https://calculator.aws/**. Accessed on: 10 out. 2023.

ARMBRUST, M. et al. (2010). A View of Cloud Computing. Communications of the ACM, v. 53, n. 4, p. 50-58.

BELKIN, N.J. (1978). Information concepts for information science. Journal of Documentation, v. 34, n. 1, p. 55-85.

BOLLIER, D., & Firestone, C. M. (2010). The promise and peril of Big Data. Washington, DC: Aspen Institute, Communications and Society Program.

BOYD, D; CRAWFORD, K. (2012). Critical Questions for Big Data: Provocations for a Cultural, Technological, and Scholarly Phenomenon. Information, Communication, & Society v.15, n.5, p. 662-679.

CHENG, Y., Qin, C., & RUSU, F. (2012). Big Data Analytics made easy. SIGMOD '12 Proceedings of the 2012 ACM SIGMOD International Conference on Management of Data New York.

COHEN, J.E. (2012). Configuring the Networked Self. Law, Code, and the Play of Everyday Practice. Yale University Press.

GLASS, R. ; CALLAHAN, (2015).S. The Big Data-Driven Business: How to Use Big Data to Win Customers, Beat Competitors, and Boost Profit. New Jersey: John Wiley & Sons, Inc.

GOOGLE CLOUD. (2023). Cloud Pricing. Available at: **https://cloud.google.com/pricing**. Accessed on: 10 out. 2023.

IBM. (2014). Exploiting Big Data in telecommunications to increase revenue, reduce customer churn and operating costs. Source: IBM: http://www-01.ibm.com/software/data/bigdata/industry-telco.html.

INMON, W. H. (1996). Building the Data Warehouse. John Wiley & Sons, New Yorkm NY, USA.2nd edition.

INTERNATIONAL ORGANIZATION FOR STANDARDIZATION. (2015). ISO/IEC 27040:2015 - Information technology — Security techniques — Storage security. Geneva: ISO.

JARVELIN, K. & Vakkari, P. (1993) The evolution of Library and Information Science 1965-1985: a content analysis of journal articles. Information Processing & Management, v.29, n.1, p. 129-144.

KAMIOKA, T; TAPANAINEN, T. (2014). Organizational use of Big Data and competitive advantage - Exploration of Antecedents. Available   at: https://www.researchgate.net/publication/284551664_Organiz ational_Use_of_Big_Data_and_Competitive_Advantage_- _Exploration_of_Antecedents.

MELL, P.; GRANCE, T. (2011). The NIST Definition of Cloud Computing. National Institute of Standards and Technology, Special Publication 800-145.

MICROSOFT AZURE. (2023). Azure Pricing Calculator. Available at: **https://azure.microsoft.com/en-us/pricing/calculator/**. Accessed on: 10 out. 2023.

PAVLO, A., PAULSON, E., RASIN, A., ABADI, D. J., DEWITT, D. J., MADDEN, S., & STONEBRAKER, M. (2009). A comparison of approaches to large-scale data analysis. SIGMOD, pp. 165–178.

RAJ, P., & DEKA, G. C. (2012). Handbook of Research on Cloud Infrastructures for Big Data Analytics. Information Science: IGI Global.

ROHS DIRECTIVE. (2011). Directive 2011/65/EU of the European Parliament and of the Council on the restriction of the use of certain hazardous substances in electrical and electronic equipment. Brussels: European Union.

SMITH, R.; JONES, T. (2018). Data Destruction: Best Practices for Secure Data Disposal. Journal of Information Security, v. 12, n. 3, p. 45-60.

SUBRAMANIAM, Anushree. 2020. What is Big Data? – A Beginner's Guide to the World of Big Data. Available at: edureka.co/blog/what-is-big-data/.

TAYLOR, M.; HURLEY, D. (2016). Cloudonomics: The Business Value of Cloud Computing. Wiley.

WANG, Y., KUNG, L., & BYRD, T. A. (2018). Big Data analytics: Understanding its capabilities and potential benefits for healthcare organizations. Technological Forecasting and Social Change, 126, 3-13.

WIDJAYA, Ivan. (2019). What are the costs of big data? Available at: **http://www.smbceo.com/2019/09/04/what-are-the-costs-of-big-data/**

WORLD ECONOMIC FORUM. (2020). The Global Risks Report 2020. Geneva: WEF.

11 Big Data Collection: Unlocking the Future of Data in an Essential Collection.

The Big Data collection was created to be an indispensable guide for professionals, students, and enthusiasts who want to confidently navigate the vast and fascinating universe of data. In an increasingly digital and interconnected world, Big Data is not just a tool, but a fundamental strategy for the transformation of businesses, processes, and decisions. This collection sets out to simplify complex concepts and empower your readers to turn data into valuable insights.

Each volume in the collection addresses an essential component of this area, combining theory and practice to offer a broad and integrated understanding. You'll find themes such as:

In addition to exploring the fundamentals, the collection also looks into the future, with discussions on emerging trends such as the integration of artificial intelligence, text analytics, and governance in increasingly dynamic and global environments.

Whether you're a manager looking for ways to optimize processes, a data scientist exploring new techniques, or a beginner curious to understand the impact of data on everyday life, the Big Data collection is the ideal partner on this journey. Each book has been developed with accessible yet technically sound language, allowing readers of all levels to advance their understanding and skills.

Get ready to master the power of data and stand out in an ever-evolving market. The Big Data collection is available on Amazon and is the key to unlocking the future of data-driven intelligence.

11.1   Who is the Big Data collection for.

The Big Data collection is designed to cater to a diverse audience that shares the goal of understanding and applying the power of data in an increasingly information-driven world. Whether you're a seasoned professional or just starting your journey in the technology and data space, this collection offers valuable insights, practical examples, and indispensable tools.

1. Technology and Data Professionals.

Data scientists, data engineers, analysts, and developers will find in the collection the fundamentals they need to master concepts such as Big Data Analytics, distributed computing, Hadoop, and advanced tools. Each volume covers technical topics in a practical way, with clear explanations and examples that can be applied in everyday life.

2. Managers and Organizational Leaders.

For leaders and managers, the collection offers a strategic view on how to implement and manage Big Data projects. The books show how to use data to optimize processes, identify opportunities, and make informed decisions. Real-world examples illustrate how companies have used Big Data to transform their businesses in industries such as retail, healthcare, and the environment.

3. Entrepreneurs and Small Businesses.

Entrepreneurs and small business owners who want to leverage the power of data to improve their competitiveness can also benefit. The collection presents practical strategies for using Big Data in a scalable way, demystifying the idea that this technology is exclusive to large corporations.

4. Students and Beginners in the Area.

If you're a student or just starting to explore the universe of Big Data, this collection is the perfect starting point. With accessible language and practical examples, the books make complex concepts more understandable, preparing you to dive deeper into data science and artificial intelligence.

5. Curious and Technology Enthusiasts.

For those who, even outside of the corporate or academic environment, have an interest in understanding how Big Data is shaping the world, the collection offers a fascinating and educational introduction. Discover how data is transforming areas as diverse as health, sustainability, and human behavior.

Regardless of your level of expertise or the industry you're in, the Big Data collection is designed to empower your readers with actionable insights, emerging trends, and a comprehensive view of the future of data. If you're looking to understand and apply the power of Big Data to grow professionally or transform your business, this collection is for you. Available on Amazon, it is the essential guide to mastering the impact of data in the digital age.

11.2   Get to know the books in the Collection.

11.2.1 Simplifying Big Data into 7 Chapters.

This book is an essential guide for anyone who wants to understand and apply the fundamental concepts of Big Data in a clear and practical way. In a straightforward and accessible format, the book covers everything from theoretical pillars, such as the 5 Vs of Big Data, to modern tools and techniques, including Hadoop and Big Data Analytics.

Exploring real examples and strategies applicable in areas such as health, retail, and the environment, this work is ideal for technology professionals, managers, entrepreneurs, and students looking to transform data into valuable insights.

With an approach that connects theory and practice, this book is the perfect starting point for mastering the Big Data universe and leveraging its possibilities.

11.2.2 Big Data Management.

This book offers a practical and comprehensive approach to serving a diverse audience, from beginner analysts to experienced managers, students, and entrepreneurs.

With a focus on the efficient management of large volumes of information, this book presents in-depth analysis, real-world examples, comparisons between technologies such as Hadoop and Apache Spark, and practical strategies to avoid pitfalls and drive success.

Each chapter is structured to provide applicable insights, from the fundamentals to advanced analytics tools.

11.2.3 Big Data Architecture.

This book is intended for a diverse audience, including data architects who need to build robust platforms, analysts who want to understand how data layers integrate, and executives who are looking to inform informed decisions. Students and researchers in computer science, data engineering, and management will also find here a solid and up-to-date reference.

The content combines a practical approach and conceptual rigor. You'll be guided from the fundamentals, such as the 5 Vs of Big Data, to the complexity of layered architectures, spanning infrastructure, security, analytics tools, and storage standards like Data Lake and Data Warehouse. In addition, clear examples, real case studies, and technology comparisons will help turn theoretical knowledge into practical applications and effective strategies.

11.2.4 Big Data Implementation.

This volume has been carefully crafted to be a practical and accessible guide, connecting theory to practice for professionals and students who want to master the strategic implementation of Big Data solutions.

It covers everything from quality analysis and data integration to topics such as real-time processing, virtualization, security, and governance, offering clear and applicable examples.

11.2.5 Strategies to Reduce Costs and Maximize Big Data Investments.

With a practical and reasoned approach, this book offers detailed analysis, real case studies and strategic solutions for IT managers, data analysts, entrepreneurs and business professionals.

This book is an indispensable guide to understanding and optimizing the costs associated with implementing Big Data, covering everything from storage and processing to small business-specific strategies and cloud cost analysis.

As part of the "Big Data" collection, it connects to other volumes that deeply explore the technical and strategic dimensions of the field, forming an essential library for anyone seeking to master the challenges and opportunities of the digital age.

11.2.6 700 Big Data Questions Collection.

This collection is designed to provide dynamic, challenging, and hands-on learning. With 700 questions strategically crafted and distributed in 5 volumes, it allows you to advance in the domain of Big Data in a progressive and engaging way. Each answer is an opportunity to expand your vision and apply concepts realistically and effectively.

The collection consists of the following books:

1   BIG DATA: 700 Questions - Volume 1.

It deals with information as the raw material for everything, the fundamental concepts and applications of Big Data.

2   BIG DATA: 700 Questions - Volume 2.

It addresses Big Data in the context of information science, data technology trends and analytics, Augmented analytics, continuous intelligence, distributed computing, and latency.

3   BIG DATA: 700 Questions - Volume 3.

It contemplates the technological and management aspects of Big Data, data mining, classification trees, logistic regression and professions in the context of Big Data.

4   BIG DATA: 700 Questions - Volume 4.

It deals with the requirements for Big Data management, the data structures used, the architecture and storage layers, Business Intelligence in the context of Big Data, and application virtualization.

5   BIG DATA: 700 Questions - Volume 5.

The book deals with SAAS, IAAS AND PAAS, Big Data implementation, overhead and hidden costs, Big Data for small businesses, digital security and data warehousing in the context of Big Data.

11.2.7 Big Data Glossary.

As large-scale data becomes the heart of strategic decisions in a variety of industries, this book offers a bridge between technical jargon and practical clarity, allowing you to turn complex information into valuable insights.

With clear definitions, practical examples, and intuitive organization, this glossary is designed to cater to a wide range of readers – from developers and data engineers to managers and the curious looking to explore the transformative impact of Big Data in their fields.

12 Discover the "Artificial Intelligence and the Power of Data" Collection – An Invitation to Transform Your Career and Knowledge.

The "Artificial Intelligence and the Power of Data" Collection was created for those who want not only to understand Artificial Intelligence (AI), but also to apply it strategically and practically.

In a series of carefully crafted volumes, I unravel complex concepts in a clear and accessible manner, ensuring the reader has a thorough understanding of AI and its impact on modern societies.

No matter your level of familiarity with the topic, this collection turns the difficult into the didactic, the theoretical into the applicable, and the technical into something powerful for your career.

12.1   Why buy this collection?

We are living through an unprecedented technological revolution, where AI is the driving force in areas such as medicine, finance, education, government, and entertainment.

The collection "Artificial Intelligence and the Power of Data" dives deep into all these sectors, with practical examples and reflections that go far beyond traditional concepts.

You'll find both the technical expertise and the ethical and social implications of AI encouraging you to see this technology not just as a tool, but as a true agent of transformation.

Each volume is a fundamental piece of this innovative puzzle: from machine learning to data governance and from ethics to practical application.

With the guidance of an experienced author who combines academic research with years of hands-on practice, this collection is more than a set of books – it's an indispensable guide for anyone looking to navigate and excel in this burgeoning field.

12.2   Target Audience of this Collection?

This collection is for everyone who wants to play a prominent role in the age of AI:

- ✓ Tech Professionals: Receive deep technical insights to expand their skills.

- ✓ Students and the Curious: have access to clear explanations that facilitate the understanding of the complex universe of AI.

- ✓ Managers, business leaders, and policymakers will also benefit from the strategic vision on AI, which is essential for making well-informed decisions.

- ✓ Professionals in Career Transition: Professionals in career transition or interested in specializing in AI will find here complete material to build their learning trajectory.

12.3   Much More Than Technique – A Complete Transformation.

This collection is not just a series of technical books; It is a tool for intellectual and professional growth.

With it, you go far beyond theory: each volume invites you to a deep reflection on the future of humanity in a world where machines and algorithms are increasingly present.

This is your invitation to master the knowledge that will define the future and become part of the transformation that Artificial Intelligence brings to the world.

Be a leader in your industry, master the skills the market demands, and prepare for the future with the "Artificial Intelligence and the Power of Data" collection.

This is not just a purchase; It is a decisive investment in your learning and professional development journey.

13 The Books of the Collection.

13.1 Data, Information and Knowledge in the era of Artificial Intelligence.

This book essentially explores the theoretical and practical foundations of Artificial Intelligence, from data collection to its transformation into intelligence. It focuses primarily on machine learning, AI training, and neural networks.

13.2 From Data to Gold: How to Turn Information into Wisdom in the Age of AI.

This book offers critical analysis on the evolution of Artificial Intelligence, from raw data to the creation of artificial wisdom, integrating neural networks, deep learning, and knowledge modeling.

It presents practical examples in health, finance, and education, and addresses ethical and technical challenges.

13.3 Challenges and Limitations of Data in AI.

The book offers an in-depth analysis of the role of data in the development of AI exploring topics such as quality, bias, privacy, security, and scalability with practical case studies in healthcare, finance, and public safety.

13.4   Historical Data in Databases for AI: Structures, Preservation, and Purge.

This book investigates how historical data management is essential to the success of AI projects. It addresses the relevance of ISO standards to ensure quality and safety, in addition to analyzing trends and innovations in data processing.

13.5   Controlled Vocabulary for Data Dictionary: A Complete Guide.

This comprehensive guide explores the advantages and challenges of implementing controlled vocabularies in the context of AI and information science. With a detailed approach, it covers everything from the naming of data elements to the interactions between semantics and cognition.

13.6   Data Curation and Management for the Age of AI.

This book presents advanced strategies for transforming raw data into valuable insights, with a focus on meticulous curation and efficient data management. In addition to technical solutions, it addresses ethical and legal issues, empowering the reader to face the complex challenges of information.

13.7   Information Architecture.

The book addresses data management in the digital age, combining theory and practice to create efficient and scalable AI systems, with insights into modeling and ethical and legal challenges.

13.8   Fundamentals: The   Essentials   of   Mastering   Artificial   Intelligence.

An essential work for anyone who wants to master the key concepts of AI, with an accessible approach and practical examples. The book explores innovations such as Machine Learning and Natural Language

Processing, as well as ethical and legal challenges, and offers a clear view of the impact of AI on various industries.

13.9   LLMS - Large-Scale Language Models.

This essential guide helps you understand the revolution of Large-Scale Language Models (LLMs) in AI.

The book explores the evolution of GPTs and the latest innovations in human-computer interaction, offering practical insights into their impact on industries such as healthcare, education, and finance.

13.10   Machine Learning: Fundamentals and Advances.

This book offers a comprehensive overview of supervised and unsupervised algorithms, deep neural networks, and federated learning. In addition to addressing issues of ethics and explainability of models.

13.11   Inside Synthetic Minds.

This book reveals how these 'synthetic minds' are redefining creativity, work, and human interactions. This work presents a detailed analysis of the challenges and opportunities provided by these technologies, exploring their profound impact on society.

13.12   The Issue of Copyright.

This book invites the reader to explore the future of creativity in a world where human-machine collaboration is a reality, addressing questions about authorship, originality, and intellectual property in the age of generative AIs.

13.13   1121 Questions and Answers: From Basic to Complex – Part 1 to 4.

Organized into four volumes, these questions serve as essential practical guides to mastering key AI concepts.

Part 1 addresses information, data, geoprocessing, the evolution of artificial intelligence, its historical milestones and basic concepts.

Part 2 delves into complex concepts such as machine learning, natural language processing, computer vision, robotics, and decision algorithms.

Part 3 addresses issues such as data privacy, work automation, and the impact of large-scale language models (LLMs).

Part 4 explores the central role of data in the age of artificial intelligence, delving into the fundamentals of AI and its applications in areas such as mental health, government, and anti-corruption.

13.14   The Definitive Glossary of Artificial Intelligence.

This glossary presents more than a thousand artificial intelligence concepts clearly explained, covering topics such as Machine Learning, Natural Language Processing, Computer Vision, and AI Ethics.

- Part 1 contemplates concepts starting with the letters A to D.
- Part 2 contemplates concepts initiated by the letters E to M.
- Part 3 contemplates concepts starting with the letters N to Z.

13.15   Prompt Engineering - Volumes 1 to 6.

This collection covers all the fundamentals of prompt engineering, providing a complete foundation for professional development.

With a rich variety of prompts for areas such as leadership, digital marketing, and information technology, it offers practical examples to improve clarity, decision-making, and gain valuable insights.

The volumes cover the following subjects:

- Volume 1: Fundamentals. Structuring Concepts and History of Prompt Engineering.
- Volume 2: Security and Privacy in AI.

- Volume 3: Language Models, Tokenization, and Training Methods.
- Volume 4: How to Ask Right Questions.
- Volume 5: Case Studies and Errors.
- Volume 6: The Best Prompts.

13.16 Guide to Being a Prompt Engineer – Volumes 1 and 2.

The collection explores the advanced fundamentals and skills required to be a successful prompt engineer, highlighting the benefits, risks, and the critical role this role plays in the development of artificial intelligence.

Volume 1 covers crafting effective prompts, while Volume 2 is a guide to understanding and applying the fundamentals of Prompt Engineering.

13.17 Data Governance with AI – Volumes 1 to 3.

Find out how to implement effective data governance with this comprehensive collection. Offering practical guidance, this collection covers everything from data architecture and organization to protection and quality assurance, providing a complete view to transform data into strategic assets.

Volume 1 addresses practices and regulations. Volume 2 explores in depth the processes, techniques, and best practices for conducting effective audits on data models. Volume 3 is your definitive guide to deploying data governance with AI.

13.18 Algorithm Governance.

This book looks at the impact of algorithms on society, exploring their foundations and addressing ethical and regulatory issues. It addresses transparency, accountability, and bias, with practical solutions for auditing and monitoring algorithms in sectors such as finance, health, and education.

13.19 From IT Professional to AI Expert: The Ultimate Guide to a Successful Career Transition.

For Information Technology professionals, the transition to AI represents a unique opportunity to enhance skills and contribute to the development of innovative solutions that shape the future.

In this book, we investigate the reasons for making this transition, the essential skills, the best learning path, and the prospects for the future of the IT job market.

13.20 Intelligent Leadership with AI: Transform Your Team and Drive Results.

This book reveals how artificial intelligence can revolutionize team management and maximize organizational performance.

By combining traditional leadership techniques with AI-powered insights, such as predictive analytics-based leadership, you'll learn how to optimize processes, make more strategic decisions, and create more efficient and engaged teams.

13.21 Impacts and Transformations: Complete Collection.

This collection offers a comprehensive and multifaceted analysis of the transformations brought about by Artificial Intelligence in contemporary society.

- Volume 1: Challenges and Solutions in the Detection of Texts Generated by Artificial Intelligence.
- Volume 2: The Age of Filter Bubbles. Artificial Intelligence and the Illusion of Freedom.
- Volume 3: Content Creation with AI - How to Do It?
- Volume 4: The Singularity Is Closer Than You Think.

- Volume 5: Human Stupidity versus Artificial Intelligence.
- Volume 6: The Age of Stupidity! A Cult of Stupidity?
- Volume 7: Autonomy in Motion: The Intelligent Vehicle Revolution.
- Volume 8: Poiesis and Creativity with AI.
- Volume 9: Perfect Duo: AI + Automation.
- Volume 10: Who Holds the Power of Data?

13.22   Big Data with AI: Complete Collection.

The collection covers everything from the technological fundamentals and architecture of Big Data to the administration and glossary of essential technical terms.

The collection also discusses the future of humanity's relationship with the enormous volume of data generated in the databases of training in Big Data structuring.

- Volume 1: Fundamentals.
- Volume 2: Architecture.
- Volume 3: Implementation.
- Volume 4: Administration.
- Volume 5: Essential Themes and Definitions.
- Volume 6: Data Warehouse, Big Data, and AI.

14 About the Author.

I'm Marcus Pinto, better known as Prof. Marcão, a specialist in information technology, information architecture and artificial intelligence.

With more than four decades of dedicated work and research, I have built a solid and recognized trajectory, always focused on making technical knowledge accessible and applicable to all those who seek to understand and stand out in this transformative field.

My experience spans strategic consulting, education and authorship, as well as an extensive performance as an information architecture analyst.

This experience enables me to offer innovative solutions adapted to the constantly evolving needs of the technological market, anticipating trends and creating bridges between technical knowledge and practical impact.

Over the years, I have developed comprehensive and in-depth expertise in data, artificial intelligence, and information governance –

areas that have become essential for building robust and secure systems capable of handling the vast volume of data that shapes today's world.

My book collection, available on Amazon, reflects this expertise, addressing topics such as Data Governance, Big Data, and Artificial Intelligence with a clear focus on practical applications and strategic vision.

Author of more than 150 books, I investigate the impact of artificial intelligence in multiple spheres, exploring everything from its technical bases to the ethical issues that become increasingly urgent with the adoption of this technology on a large scale.

In my lectures and mentorships, I share not only the value of AI, but also the challenges and responsibilities that come with its implementation – elements that I consider essential for ethical and conscious adoption.

I believe that technological evolution is an inevitable path. My books are a proposed guide on this path, offering deep and accessible insights for those who want not only to understand, but to master the technologies of the future.

With a focus on education and human development, I invite you to join me on this transformative journey, exploring the possibilities and challenges that this digital age has in store for us.

15 How to Contact Prof. Marcão.

15.1 For lectures, training and business mentoring.

marcao.tecno@gmail.com

15.2 Prof. Marcão, on Linkedin.

https://bit.ly/linkedin_profmarcao

www.ingramcontent.com/pod-product-compliance
Lightning Source LLC
Chambersburg PA
CBHW071007050326
40689CB00014B/3530